2 Losses
1 Divine Gift

DERRA BYRD

WestBow
PRESS
A DIVISION OF THOMAS NELSON

ISBN: 978-1-4497-4492-2 (sc)
ISBN: 978-1-4497-4493-9 (e)

Library of Congress Control Number: 2012905539

WestBow Press books may be ordered through booksellers or by contacting:

WestBow Press
A Division of Thomas Nelson
1663 Liberty Drive
Bloomington, IN 47403
www.westbowpress.com
1-(866) 928-1240

Printed in the United States of America

WestBow Press rev. date: 3/28/2012

Chapter 1:

RIVER RUNS WILD

The summer had been under way for several months. It was not only the hottest summer, but it was about to be the most exciting summer. My husband Jason and I had officially decided to start a family. This is something that I had wanted for a long time. We were in our own home. We had been married almost nine years. We felt that we were ready for the responsibility of a child. Key word "we" felt that we were ready to embark on the new adventure.

Up to this point, we craved that bond that parents share with their children. We had both grew up in divorced homes, and we both agreed that we never wanted our children to experience that. Divorce had devastated both of our families. In a sense, this idea of divorce not being an option had brought us together with a mutual understanding that we were committed to each other. We wanted to be stable and provide a loving home for a child. Thankfully, our years of being immature and selfish had all come to an end, and we were embarking on a journey to create a life and a home environment that we both never had.

The weekend that we decided to officially start our trek for a child, we embarked on a rafting trip down the Ocoee River. The trip symbolized our last "hoorah" before our lives would change completely. I was so nervous about the trip that I could barely eat that morning. Jason was the adventurous type. I, in my younger days, was very adventurous. However, being married and becoming an adult, I was more aware of the consequences that could occur in getting hurt.

Worrying was something that I was guilty of. This trip was a prime example of my biggest fear which was being hurt or something happening to me. Growing up, my mother was a nurse. I was constantly around the medical environment. So, by the time I was in middle school, I could recite the protocols of a heart attack. I was always attentive to my body and its every function. This phase really didn't control me until I married and moved in with Jason. We were miles away from my family. I was alone and on my own. I had several bouts of panic attacks. They were so bad that at points I would completely feel like I was having a heart attack.

I remember several nights where I couldn't sleep because my heart would be racing. My husband would be sound asleep in our bed while I would be shaking all over with fear. Afraid that he would think I was a freak of some sort, I would lie there in silence just praying to the Lord to calm me down and help me sleep. There would always be a calmness that would come over me as I was praying for the Lord's help.

These panic attacks didn't just occur at home. They even occurred as I was driving. I remember one instance where I was driving home from college, and I had one of the worst panic attacks that I had ever had. I just remember begging God to help me and pleading for this worrying to go away.

In most cases of my panic attacks, I would call my mother and cry to her, and she would reassure me that everything was okay. I didn't realize at the time, but God was trying to tell me that I needed him and no one else. Yes, I could call my mother for reassurance in the doom that I was dreaming up in my head, but it was only a temporary peace that she could give me. I needed a permanent peace that only God could give me. God showed me that if I put my true faith in him alone and not of the world, that I would never be alone in this life. He would give me a peace that I would never be able to explain or understand.

This was the kind of peace that was only given by God. It's a peace that no reassuring human being could give. That path for peace would forever change my life. I praise God for that peace that he gave me. When the world around me told me to take medicine to take away the worries, God reminded me that he made the world and created life. God reminded me that he sent his son Jesus to die on a cross and conquer the world of sin. If God could do all this, anxiety was a walk in the park for Him. All I needed was Faith. Faith is such a simple word, but putting that word into use is something that changed my life forever. I forever owe my happiness to God for all that he has brought me through.

At the time that this worrying started, I thought "why me?" Little did I know that God was teaching me something that some people didn't even get to experience in their entire lives. All the tears and times of fear were so worth the ride that I had experienced with God. That time in my life reminded me of a few verses out of the book of James. James 1: 2-4 says " My brethren, count it all joy when ye fall into divers temptations; Knowing this, that the trying of your faith worketh patience. But let patience have her perfect work, that ye may be perfect and entire, wanting nothing."(KJV) Patience and maturity in my walk with the Lord is exactly what I needed. God knows exactly what we need and when we need it. This verse clearly talks about how trials can strengthen us.

I love how the verse clearly states to count our trials as joy. I seldom counted my panic attacks as joy at the time. However, when I really grasped the concept of what God was teaching me through these panic attack episodes, I forever have joy in my heart for those temptations and hardships.

Patience as mentioned in the verses of James does not just mean waiting. It means to actually wait and know that God is in control. This lesson is something that I am truly grateful to have learned.

There were times in my life that I still had to remind myself of what I had been through. As a Christian, I still struggled at times with worrying. I had, at points, let myself fit into that old mind-frame. God helps us, but we also have to do our part. I expected God to do everything, but I had to put in work as well. So, sometimes I would let my sinful self get lazy and start worrying again.

The rafting trip was no exception. That weekend the same worry that I had worked on getting over tried to creep into my mind. I start praying before we hit the river. The river that we were rafting was at one point home of some of the Olympic events, which tells you that it was no lazy river. It had the highest class of rapids. I was nervous and wanted to give up before we began. I realized when I stuck my foot in the water that I was committed. The river was tough that day, but God helped me through it as he always did. There were times on the river when I wanted to jump out of the boat and climb the bank to the road in an attempt to walk back.

This experience of wanting to exit the river and climb the bank to the road is a reminder of how tough life can get. Sometimes, we face hardships in life, and I always wanted to flee. However, God wants us to cast our cares on Him. We don't need to run in the opposite direction. We need to run to God and Him only. With my anxiety, I could have easily ran up the bank and tried to help myself feel better. However, I put my faith in someone solid which is God.

Once we reached the point of seeing the awaiting raft buses, I started celebrating the victory of being alive. I realized at that point that trying to get pregnant would be an adrenaline rush just like rafting the river. I couldn't wait to see the results of our first month of trying to get pregnant. Seeing those results would be like seeing the awaiting raft buses, but it would take some work to get there. On the car ride home, my husband and I felt like we had conquered the world. The fury of the river was intense, and we were safely on our way home. We decided to stop at a restaurant for a nice quiet dinner out on a patio. The weather was beautiful, and summer was slowly coming to an end. We may have conquered the river today, but we were about to embark on the river of trying to conceive. We had just stuck our feet in the water to begin the journey of pregnancy.

Chapter 2:

THE END OF THE MONTH

The first month of trying to get pregnant seemed to go by slow. I couldn't wait to break out a pregnancy test and see the results. I was nervous, but I was so excited to see if we had a baby on the way.

I was constantly aware of any changes in my body that could clue me in to whether I was pregnant or not. This was the first month that I had stopped my birth control pills. I had been on these since I was very young since my menstrual cycles were so erratic. So, my body was going through a lot of changes.

Again, I felt extremely nervous by the result of the end of this month. I still felt like I wasn't ready. I knew that just like the river I was already committed. The way that my husband beamed over the mention of a child made my heart melt. There was no way that I was going to let my fear ruin what could be a great thing. I was finally at that point in my life where my husband and I agreed that we wanted children.

God was still working on me with the worrying. However, the fear that I was left with was staying at home alone at night. Jason worked night shift one month and then he would switch to day shift the next month. I had been staying with my mom and grandparents the months that Jason would work nights. Those nights were some long nights. I always felt like I wanted to be staying at my own home and enjoying my space with my own routine. It was hard to stay away from home, but I was afraid to stay at home at night without Jason. We lived about 30 minutes away from town or civilization, as I jokingly called it. Our home was also up against a mountain. So, needless to say, I felt very isolated. Before I married Jason, I lived near the city and never had to stay by myself. So, I was definitely experiencing a "culture shock".

The Lord was trying to tell me that I needed to learn to stay by myself. He used my grandmother to do this. My grandmother would always provide the words of wisdom for the family. Nana, as I called her, was a mother figure to me. My mother was always working, and I spent a lot of time with my grandmother. My grandmother had been through so many horrible things in her life including beatings by her father and a rape that ended in a pregnancy in her early teens. These were among the few things that she had been through in her life. So, if anybody had life advice, it was definitely her. My grandmother would always have these "hunches" as people would call them. She always had a good or bad feeling about a situation before it would happen, and it was always right. Please don't get this mistaken for anything other than God talking to her through the Holy Spirit because my Nana was a Christian. These were not "psychic abilities" as some people try to say. I believe that only God can see and know our future. After all, He did create us.

My Nana knew that we were currently trying to get pregnant. She would always tell me that I need to learn to stay by myself first before I tried to get pregnant. I would always contemplate what she said, but I knew that I would deal with this when the time had come. Every time that she told me something, it would always come true. So, little did I know that she would be right again. I guess in the back of my mind I knew that she would be right, but in a way I wanted to rebel and do it my way. The Lord was speaking through her to tell me what I needed to do. I was just too stubborn to acknowledge it.

The month was progressively going by slow. I felt like a kid waiting on Christmas Day morning in the middle of July. At the time, I was working for a local Fire Department. This job kept me really busy. However, it was always in the back of my mind of whether I could really be pregnant in the first month of trying. I contemplated every day the possibility of being pregnant and how our life would be so different.

The first month was coming to an end. The weather for the month was very erratic. There were several hurricanes that had come through this year. We lived in the Northwest corner of Georgia. So, we tended to experience some bouts of rain if hurricanes came in from the Gulf. Towards the end of the month, we had one of the worst effects of a hurricane that we had ever experienced in the south. The local news channel predicted that we would have heavy rains and wind. They left little to the imagination as far as hypothesizing the magnitude of the storm. I never expected that we would experience 12 to 15 inches of rain in a single night.

The night of the floods, I knew that something wasn't quite right. This was God telling me that something was about to happen. Looking back on that night, I was almost inclined to try to stay by myself since Jason was on night shift. I thank God that I couldn't feel peaceful about it. I was pacing back in forth in my house, So, I packed up my things for the night and decided to head to my grandmother's house. My grandmother was so nurturing and warm-hearted. I always, as a child, stayed at her house. Her house was just the most wonderful and most comfortable place that I have ever stayed. It was her presence that made me feel at ease on nights that I couldn't even consider not worrying.

I was tucked in tightly in my grandmother's huge California king bed. We were watching the weather that night. The weather man couldn't even fathom what was about to be the worst flooding that we had ever experienced in our area. I never dreamed that it would be so bad. Even with the most severe flooding heading our way, I was not worried about a thing. My grandmother had that soothing effect in her voice letting me know that we were safe in her house. As the weather moved in that night, I was ready for a good night's sleep.

Waking up the morning of the flood, I really didn't realize the magnitude of rain that had fallen. I heard the weather man say that the city in which I lived in had been hit the hardest by the rainfall measuring in at around 15 inches of rain. At this point, I felt my heart sink a little bit. Our house was on a hill. So, I didn't fear any damage to it. However, we had built a man-made bridge that, at the time, would last us forever. Yes, it needed improvements, but we had just moved into our house. So, we were working on our finances and trying to figure out everything. Our bridge was designed to get us from one side of the creek to the other. The creek had always been dry. It was a deep creek with wide banks that could hold a large capacity of water. Living up next to a huge mountain, water would rush down the mountain and into the creek. The creek was designed to hold large amounts of water, but 15 inches of water at one time was over the limit.

I remember calling my husband that morning on his way home. He was anxious to get home and see the damage. It took him several routes in an attempt to get home since our area had been hit the hardest. I could hear the fear in my husband's voice on his way home. I decided that I would wait to hear from him before trying to make my way home. It seemed like hours before he called. He called to let me know that the swift water had completely washed our bridge away. This left us with no way to drive our vehicles up the driveway to get to our house. My husband was angry at the time. Who could blame him for being angry?? We had worked really hard to get moved into our new house, and a flood had made it impossible to access our house. I was a little upset by what had happened, but I was glad that our house was still okay. Plus, it was going to give us time to stay with my family. So, it wasn't as bad for me.

Despite this major setback, it was time for the big pregnancy test. It was the end of the month, and I was excited. Test night was a major night. I wanted to wait on my husband, but my mom had bought me a test. She was encouraging me to take the test just to see what it would say. My husband was working the night shift that night. So, I decided to go ahead and take it just to see what it would say. We opened up the pack of two tests. I was so nervous. Waiting five minutes for the test to process felt like eternity. The first test that I took had a faint positive line meaning I was pregnant. My mother and I must have looked at that test a million times. I was so excited. I decided to text Jason and let him know that I had a positive test. He was so excited. This was the perfect time since we had just experienced a major setback with the bridge collapsing.

Words just couldn't describe how excited I was. However, I was so nervous too. I was still dealing with the after-effects of worrying, and I still felt like I was a kid instead of an adult because of being scared to stay by myself at night. I guess you could describe my demeanor as insecure. That pretty much summed up my life. Either way, I was committed now. Here I was about to embark on the joys of motherhood. The next step was to confirm everything with my doctor. So, I set up a doctor's appointment to get established in his practice. Blood tests were performed, and it was confirmed that I was indeed pregnant. At his request, he wanted to see me back in a couple of weeks to see my progress.

I felt like King of the world coming out of the doctor's office. I couldn't wait to tell everyone that I knew that we were pregnant. I was in shock at the time. I was early pregnant, and I didn't feel pregnant. There was just a joy that I felt knowing that a little child was forming in my womb.

I had a few more visits to the doctor after the initial one, but was not expected to return until my 8th week for my scan to see the baby's heartbeat. So, the wait was on for the next visit to see my little bundle of joy.

Meanwhile, I had told my whole family, and all my coworkers. Jason had sent me flowers at work. My coworkers kept asking why he had sent flowers since it wasn't our anniversary or my birthday. So, I had to tell them the great news. After all, I was not ashamed of something as wonderful as a pregnancy. Everyone was really excited for us. I couldn't wait to see the doctor for my next visit to see the progress.

Chapter 3:

PRODUCTS OF CONCEPTION

I was officially at week 6 of my pregnancy. My body was definitely going through a lot of changes. I didn't know if this was from the pregnancy or from being off my birth control pills. I remember being at work and with every little pinch of pain reading the symptoms on the internet. Like I said before, God had taught me that He held the key to my ultimate peace. However, sometimes in an attempt to feel in control, I would try to rely on things like the internet for a quick peace. This never solved anything and usually created more drama in my head.

I had started experiencing some brown discharge similar to that of period symptoms. I was at work at the time, and I remember phoning my doctor at the time who stated that this was normal sometimes. He recommended coming in just to make sure that nothing was going on. My appointment was not until 1 pm that day. It was only 9am when I started experiencing this. I was so freaked out that the internet was the only source of comfort that I could remedy this worry for the time being. I was at work and supposed to be working hard on health insurance reports. All that I could think about was what was going on in my body. There were a lot of forums on the internet where women had experienced the same symptoms and went on to experience the dreaded "M" word. (M for Miscarriage)

The restless worries were starting to creep in more and more as the day progressed. I started experiencing major clots and cramping. I was in a lot of pain. I didn't know what to expect. I was just hoping that the "M" word was not in my vocabulary. I started to experience panic-stricken fear. I had a chat with my boss, who had already had a child. She told me that I had nothing to worry about. In the back of her mind, she knew what was happening. She just didn't want to cause more worry on top of what I was already experiencing.

I started on my way to the doctor's office. My mother was off work that day. She was worried and nervous as well. She offered to go to the doctor with me, but I told her that I would be fine. As I was driving in my car, I remember praying and telling God that whatever his plan was that I would be okay. I knew that either way God was in control.

I arrived at the doctor's office. I decided to stop into the restroom before entering the office to check the situation. I started bleeding heavily and had to put on a maxi-pad. I just knew that something was wrong. It was almost like I had come to terms with what was happening in that bathroom before I had even heard from the doctor. I walked into the office and was seated in one of the exam rooms. As soon as the doctor walked in, I could tell that he was worried as well with his concerned demeanor. He started to do an internal exam. I remember him telling the nurse as he removed things out of my vagina to label them "Products of Conception" and place them in a laboratory cup. He told me that I was miscarrying. I was seriously hurt not at the "M" word, but his choice of words. "Products of Conception" was what he called my baby. How could he say that?? This was the gift that God blessed us with. This was the sweet result of the love that me and my husband had for each other. This was the bridge that would forever connect me and my husband. This was my future son or daughter. This was more than the product of conception. Those three words were forever engrained in my mind.

The doctor finished up his internal exam and reassured me that I had done nothing wrong to cause this. He assured me that this was more common than people think. He told me how even his wife had experienced this twice before she had their first child. He asked me if I wanted any anxiety medicine to help me cope with the loss. I told him that I didn't need anything. I knew that God would be the only source of medicine that I needed. After all, He is the Great Physician.

As I walked out of the exam room, my mind was a wreck. I just kept hearing the three words that the doctor had called my baby. As I approached the front desk where they take your insurance information, I remember the lady at the front desk telling me to not forget about my appointment for my first scan of the baby. As soon as she said this, I felt like all the wind had been knocked out of me. I had set up this appointment for my 8 week mark to hear the baby's heartbeat. I remember just looking at the lady at the front desk and telling her that I wouldn't need the appointment anymore as I slowly walked off.

Then, I started my hour drive back to my mom's house. I called her on the way home and told her what had happened. My mom was a complete wreck. I had to reassure her that it would be okay. It's like God had gave me this peace and let me know that everything was okay.

The thing that I dreaded the most was telling Jason. I knew that he wanted this so bad. I was afraid that he would be mad at me and disappointed. That day was one of the longest days. I was waiting for Jason to get off work. He was on day shift at this time and didn't return home until around 7 pm. I was in pain all day, and there were lots of tears shed during the day. I needed the comfort from Jason that only he could give. He always knew how to calm me down and help me through a hard time. He finally made it home. We both shed tears. He told me that he would love me regardless. I believed him, but I felt so alone during this time. I didn't know what to do with myself. I was mortified at what happened. Plus, we had told our whole family that we were pregnant. We had to call and tell everyone what had happened. I had never experienced something so humbling as calling my family and Jason's family and telling them that our future son or daughter had passed away. I felt so disappointed in myself. This was the first time that we had been pregnant, and I felt like I had failed at life. I felt that everything up to this point in my life amounted to nothing but a failure. I thought of everything that I had done in that past month and blamed myself for this happening.

Chapter 4:

HIS TIMING

Several months had passed since my first miscarriage. I had hit a plateau of emotions. I was handling the situation bravely on the outside, but I felt breathless and helpless on the inside. I was slowly falling into depression. I had never experienced this feeling before in my life. I did something that most people do which was to start eating my pain away. I gained about 15 to 20 pounds in about 3 months. This was certainly unusual for me due to my height and genetic disposition.

I knew that the only way that I would ever get through this was by the help of God. That was the one thing that going through the worrying phase in my life taught me was that I couldn't get over anything on my own. God was always standing right beside me. He was waiting on me to ask for help. Pride would always take over me to try to handle the problem myself. By the time I failed trying to help myself, God found me in a broken state. This was something that I struggled with. My selfish side always proved itself in the face of fear by me contemplating the solution on my own. The loss of a child was no exception.

I started devouring every verse of the bible as it pertained to the emotion that I was going through. I also started getting involved heavily on teaching AWANA on Wednesday nights at my church. AWANA was a program for kids on Wednesday nights that allowed them to learn lessons pertaining to the bible, build friendships, and of course play awesome games. I was fortunate enough to have the privilege of teaching the middle school age kids. I am so thankful to God for the opportunity to teach these kids. I owe everything to God. Little did I know that by teaching these kids lessons in the bible, God was also teaching me lessons that pertained to my current state of depression and sadness over my loss.

It was through God's teaching that I was able to understand why everything had happened in my life up to this point. I mean in one single month our bridge was completely washed away leaving us to stay with family members, and our baby that we worked so hard for had slipped away before we ever got to meet it. I suddenly realized that it wasn't my timing it was His timing. Notice that the word "His" is capitalized. This means God's timing. I thought that in my life I could just snap my fingers and make everything happen. It didn't work that way. I realized that without our bridge collapsing, I would have been alone in going through this miscarriage. God allowed that to happen because he knew that I needed to have the comfort of my family to get through such a tragic time. Staying with my family at the time allowed me to focus my energy in healthy ways. Granted, I still went through a stage of depression. That was however by choice. We all have a choice on how to deal with situations. God will give you the knowledge on how to deal with it, but it is up to us to use that knowledge and how we use it.

I never really quite understood the timing of the miscarriage either. I would often feel pity on myself because that had happened to us. It was not until one of my AWANA middle school girls pulled me to the side one night that I realized why I had went through a miscarriage. She began to cry hysterically in telling me that she had miscarried during the week at the age of 12. It was at that point that I thanked God for allowing me to go through this because I was now able to help someone else who was going through this. All the sadness and depression inside of me slowly started to evaporate in that one single moment. I no longer felt the victim role. It was time for me to tell people my experience and share how God had pulled me through it. God knew that this girl was going to pull me aside at this single moment to ask for advice. God had equipped me to witness to this girl. As bad as all the events that had happened in my life were, I praised God for the opportunity to go through these events. It was worth everything to be able to experience this one witnessing opportunity.

From that point on, I realized that I needed to share my story with the world. God had helped me through a lot in my life. This was the least that I could do for Him. I also realized that the reigns that I had in my hand for my life would need to be given to God. After all, I clearly wasn't in control. God knows what we need at the moment that we need it. We can wish all day that things would be a certain way, but it is God who holds the timing. I had never really experienced that until going through this miscarriage experience. Who knew that all these events would give me great insight and understanding of God??

Chapter 5:

KENTUCKY BOUND

A few months had vanished away. Good Friday was soon approaching. At this point, I had started exercising to make myself feel healthier. I, of course, still had times where all I could think about was those events of the miscarriage. I was feeling stronger as each month passed by. I take no credit for this because God was strengthening me by his teachings and his examples. If it would have been up to me, I would still be laying in the fetal position in a dark room still sobbing. However, God knew what it would take to make me feel better and to help me learn what I needed to learn.

It was the week of Good Friday. I was feeling great. Spring was officially arriving. Warm southern weather was on its way. I was feeling a little weird and decided to take a pregnancy test. Jason and I had just decided to go at life normally. We had the "whatever happens happens" attitude. It was definitely more relaxing this way. We put way too much pressure on ourselves before then and were left with anger and bitterness at the end of each month. This way was so much more enjoyable. Everyone would always tell us that when you start trying you won't get pregnant. I thought they were crazy until I discovered the stress with trying to get pregnant. Then, I realized exactly what they were saying.

The pregnancy test was a very strong positive. I was excited, but I was also nervous given what had happened before. It's almost as if I wasn't enjoying the moment because I was still relying on the past. The first person that I called was my mother. She was so excited. I was excited too. I was just trying to be cautious as crazy as that sounds.

My husband had planned a trip to Kentucky to see a gun shoot/expo. I was a little nervous because I was worried about the heavy artillery noise and being pregnant. We decided that we should probably be on the cautious side and not attend the gun shoot. The night before we were supposed to leave for the shoot, I started bleeding. It wasn't much, but it was enough to be alarmed. I told my husband what was going on. We pretty much knew what was happening. So, we decided that taking a trip to Kentucky would be a great way to relieve some stress.

This second miscarriage was not as upsetting as the first one. The first one was devastating. By this time, I knew that God had a plan for us. I didn't quite know what that plan was, but I knew that He would bless us with a baby one of these days. God's peace is unlike any that I have ever experienced. It will calm you down in the middle of a raging storm.

The Kentucky trip went great. It definitely took my mind off of what was happening to my body. It may sound crazy, but the whole time I was hoping that the bleeding would go away. I knew that it wouldn't. I spotted the whole time on the trip. I decided that I better get to the doctor when I returned home. I had been through this song and dance before and knew that it wouldn't be a good result. However, I always held out hope.

Upon returning home, reality was setting in. I decided that I needed to make a doctor's appointment. I wasn't exactly thrilled about the prospect of entering the same office where several months ago our child was labeled "Product of Conception". However, I knew that I had to face the music. The doctor drew some blood-work and confirmed that I was indeed pregnant. The nurse called me to tell me the great news. However, as soon as I walked out of the doctor's office the day of the appointment, I had started a regular period. So, needless to say hearing from the nurse had taken me back to the emotions of the first miscarriage.

Chapter 6:

PRACTICE MAKES PERFECT

Several months had crept by since having the two miscarriages. As always, I had officially dug myself into my work and my teaching in church. I would always try to bury that hurt that I could never let go of. It was always in the back of my mind. It's almost as if you know that going through trials will prosper your growth, but the hurt and emotions will always be there. I also learned one thing about your emotions. The Devil will use your emotions to try to make you fall. My emotions got the best of me and caused havoc on our marriage. However, God pulled me through and strengthened our marriage in the turmoil that the Devil was trying to create. The Devil may try to destroy the good things that you have, but God is way more powerful than the devil. God sent his son Jesus to this earth to conquer the world. Jesus did just that. Jesus was tempted with all the things that you could possibly imagine. Jesus never sinned, and he conquered this world. So, the devil may try everything to break us down. However, Jesus conquered the world.

God had brought us through a rough patch. This rough patch really made us realize how much we loved each other. We knew that God had a plan for our lives together despite the setbacks that we had experienced. As rough as that patch was for our marriage, I wouldn't have traded the lessons that it taught us for the world. It brought us closer than I could ever imagine us to be.

My husband and I were still trying to get pregnant. We realized that with all the stress that we would just pray about it. After all, it was His timing and not ours. We did however decide to get a dog. This was definitely a gift from God. We drove two hours to get a Doberman Pincher puppy one Sunday afternoon. I never thought that a dog would be so much responsibility. It was a culture shock for me and Jason. We had only been responsible for ourselves up to this point. Now, we were responsible for another living creature. We were so surprised to see all the responsibility that a little puppy required. We just thought that we had been prepared for a child. I praised God for this little puppy. He was so sweet. He brought me and Jason so much joy. It was almost as if he was our child. We had so much love for him. He also brought me and Jason so much closer. Our dog was also spoiled. We often joked many times that this was his house, and we just lived here. He was and still is a blessing in our life.

At the time that we bought him, I was staying by myself at night while Jason was at work. I could never quite sleep peacefully at night. It was as if I was trying to sleep and listen for any strange noises as well. As soon as we got our puppy, staying home alone was so much easier. He was my ears while I was sleeping peacefully at night. He was a great watch-dog. He also kept me company when I felt lonely at night. I praise God for this sweet dog. He has brought us nothing but love. He has been such a blessing.

It might sound crazy, but our dog was practice for me and Jason in how to raise a child. We just thought that we knew how to be good parents. It wasn't until getting the dog that our skills were tested. There was some up and down times to raising this dog. However, we learned so much from having him. Those skills would help us in the future in raising our child.

Chapter 7:

FAITH

$\mathcal{I}$ really feel that the Lord has laid a message about Faith on my heart in writing this book. I always felt that I knew what Faith meant. In all actuality, I knew what the word Faith meant, but I wasn't putting it to action in my own life. The definition of the word faith is reliance, loyalty and complete trust in. I never realized that this was an area in my life that needed a divine intervention. I now realized that in order for me to put my faith into action, I had to experience all that I had been through. Our experiences are our teachers. God knew what it would take to prosper me as he does everyone else. God showed me a verse in the book of James. James 2: 17 said "Even so faith, if it hath no works, is dead being alone." This is such a short and powerful verse. See my faith was without action. It was almost as if my faith was dead and needed to be revived. Going through all the miscarriages and setbacks made me realize that my faith needed action. Before going through these experiences, I would tell people that I had faith until those stormy waters of life would bring me to my knees. Then, I would be left lifeless and in need of oxygen. My faith would be tossed back and forth. I realized that God was the only one that could bring me through any situation in my life. I know that I have mentioned this several times throughout the book, but I want you to get a hold of this. With that said, we had to exercise that faith and put our total reliance on God. We can't just say I have faith and then worry about it. That is taking our problem back from God. Psalms 55:22 says "Cast thy burden upon the Lord, and he shall sustain thee: he shall never suffer the righteous to be moved." If God sent Jesus to conquer this world and he did, then what makes us think that our problems are too big for him??

I struggled with this for several years especially during the worrying phases of my life. I would tell God to take the worrying away. Then, it wouldn't be 20 minutes later that I would start worrying again. It was the control issue that I couldn't get over. We are taught everyday that we are in control of our lives. We are living a lie every day. I was living this lie for a long time. Losing two children, I realized quickly that I was not in control. I also realized and praised God that I wasn't in control. Looking back at everything that happened, God knew that the timing of my desires were not the right time.

I want to make something perfectly clear. God does not punish us. God never has. Yes, I went through these situations because I needed to be strengthened in my faith. However, God did not punish me by going through this. We are all sinners. Our sins punish us. If you look back at the story of Adam and Eve, God plainly told Adam and Eve that they could eat from the trees in the garden except for the tree in the middle. God told them not to eat from this tree. This was a simple commandment. Adam and Eve were tempted by the serpent, and that is how the fall of man started. It was Adam and Eve that allowed sin into their lives. As a result, their sins punished them. We are just like Adam and Eve in that we are all sinners, and we all allow sin into our own lives by our choices or "free will".

There are situations that arise in our life that God allows to come into our lives. 1 Corinthians 10:13 states "There hath no temptation taken you but such as is common to man: but God is faithful, who will not suffer you to be tempted above that ye are able; but will with temptation also make a way to escape, that ye may be able to bear it." God knows the situation before it enters our lives. God also knows clearly through this verse which ones we can bear. The verse clearly tells us that we will not encounter a situation in our life that we cannot bear. This verse, in my opinion, supports the thought that God will never punish us. In my opinion, wouldn't someone punish you by giving you something that you couldn't handle?? These two last sentences were just some thoughts from my own opinion.

In talking about Faith, I am reminded of the story of Job. What a powerful story!! Job was a regular man that feared God and shunned evil the bible teaches us. One day, Satan was roaming the earth. The Lord asked him if he had considered his servant Job. The Lord told Satan that he was blameless and upright and feared God and shunned evil. In Job 1: 10-11, Satan told the Lord "Hast not thou made an hedge about him, and about his house, and about all that he hath on every side? thou hast blessed the work of his hands, and his substance is increased in the land. But put forth thine hand now, and touch all that he hath, and he will curse thee to thy face." Remember, the Lord allows only what he knows that we can bear. The Lord knew that whatever challenges that Satan threw at Job, he could bear it and still be faithful to the Lord. In summary, Job lost everything that he had including his children and his flocks and herds. Job had nothing. Never once did he curse at the Lord. What a true act of Faith. Job lived the meaning of Faith. After Job had endured the Devil's challenges, the Lord blessed him. In Luke 18: 29-30, it states "And he said unto them verily I say unto you, There is no man that hath left house or parents, or brethren, or wife, or children, for the Kingdom of God's sake, Who shall not receive manifold more in this present time, and in the world to come life everlasting."Jesus was telling us in the scripture that sometimes we face sacrifices to follow him, but we as believers will be repaid in this life as well as in the next, eternity.

Job was repaid with more herds and flocks than he could ever imagine. The bible even mentions that Job went on to have more children. The bible mentions that there was none more beautiful than his daughters.

As I reflect back on Job's life, I think about my own hardships. Mine were none in comparison with Job's. However, they left me with a lasting impression like that of Job. It helped me realize that all I needed was Faith in God. It taught me that nothing else in this life mattered if I didn't have Faith and use it. Happily, my story ends just like Job's. God has graciously repaid our hardships with a baby boy. I am happy to report that I am 36 weeks along with a healthy baby boy. This is by the grace of God. God knew what it would take to get to this point in my life. Praise God for everything that he has took me through to get to where I am today. God not only gave me the divine gift of faith, but also the gift of a baby. For that, I want to say thank you. I may have experienced 2 losses, but I gained a divine gift.

Chapter 8:

WHO IS HE??

I am so thankful that I had the opportunity to write this book. God has truly blessed me beyond belief. You may be asking yourself who is God that she keeps talking about?? You may be also asking why does she mention Him so much??

God is the creator of the world. God is a picture of perfection. The fall of man took place with the story of Adam and Eve and their disobedience. That is how sin entered the world. We are all sinners. Romans 3:23 states "For all have sinned, and come short of the glory of God."

Before the arrival of Jesus on this earth, people would sacrifice animals if they sinned. God knew that we needed an ultimate sacrifice to cover all of our sins. God sent Jesus, his son, to be our ultimate sacrifice. Jesus lived on this earth for 33 years. He never committed a sin. He was even tempted by everything imaginable. Jesus was crucified on a cross even though he committed no sin. In Jesus's last moments before dying on the cross he told God in Luke 23: 34 "Father, forgive them; for they know not what they do." Jesus was asking forgiveness for us. Jesus paid the way for us as sinners to have forgiveness for our sins. Jesus might have died on that cross, but He is alive and in Heaven with God. He rose from the dead 3 days later.

How do we get this forgiveness?? How does God look on us and not see our sins?? We have to accept Jesus as our Savior. Accepting Jesus as our Savior is very simple. People try to overcomplicate this. Romans 10: 9-10 states " That if thou shalt confess with thy mouth the Lord Jesus, and shalt believe in thine heart that God hath raised him from the dead, thou shalt be saved. For with the heart man believeth unto righteousness; and with the mouth confession is made unto salvation." This is so simple. Confess and believe are all that we have to do. By simply praying to God and confessing that you are sinner and believing that He sent his son Jesus to die on a cross, you will be saved. This is so simple. There is no right or wrong prayer. If you pray to God and believe in your heart, you will be saved. Romans 10:13 says "For whosoever shall call upon the name of the Lord shall be saved." This verse clearly states that everyone who calls on the name of the

Lord will have salvation. It doesn't say if you say a certain prayer. There are so many people that try to add things to this verse. I believe in what the bible says.

I remember the day that I got saved. I was 16 years old. I was going through some hard things in my life including the divorce of my parents. There was a program being offered at the church that I was attending. This program was a Christian counselor based program that allowed me to talk about my feelings regarding the divorce of my parents. The Christian Counselor that I was seeing asked me if I had ever accepted Jesus as my Savior. I froze when he asked me that. I told him "No, I will do it later." He looked at me very carefully and explained that if I didn't except Jesus as my savior that my eternity would be a place called Hell. I remember him telling me that if I left from the counseling session that day and had a wreck and was killed that I would die and go to Hell.

I kept thinking about that on the way home from the counseling session. Praise God that He kept us safe on the way home. I was riding with my mom in the car when I started crying hysterically. I told her that I wanted to go back and get saved. My mom took me back to church, and I accepted Jesus as my savior that day. I will never forget the feeling I had the day that I got saved. It is a feeling that feels like your whole body is being lifted up as you are sitting there at the altar. It is an amazing feeling that only God can give you. It feels like a fresh start. You are able to love like you have never known before. You are able to see the things that God wants you to see. It was the best decision that I have and will ever make.

I do want to say that you do not have to go to a church to be saved. You can pray right where you are right now and ask to be saved. You can pray a simple prayer like this to be saved:

Lord, I am a sinner. Please forgive me of my sins and come into my heart and save me. I believe that you sent your son Jesus to die on a cross to forgive me of my sins.

This prayer is just a guide. There is no set prayer that you have to say. Whatever you feel that you need to pray is up to you.

I hope that if you have never received Jesus that you will really look at your life and consider it. I have been through so many things in my life that without Jesus I probably would be in a depressed state or suicidal if I had to go through them alone. When you accept Jesus Christ as your savior, you will never be alone. I am also now assured that if I die today, tomorrow, or whenever that I have a place in Heaven. In John 3:3, Jesus tells the Pharisees: "Jesus answered and said unto him, Verily, verily, I say unto thee, except a man be born again, he cannot see the kingdom of God." This verse clearly states that in order to have Heaven as our eternity that we must be born again meaning accept him as our Savior.

Chapter 9:

ABRAM

I want to dedicate this whole chapter to my wonderful son Abram. He was born on December 9, 2011. I can't imagine my life without him. As soon as I looked into his eyes when he was born, I could just feel the Lord's presence. I just want to praise the Lord for this miracle. I never knew how much I could love until he came into my life. I also want to thank the Lord for a wonderful perfect pregnancy and very easy delivery. This was due to the Lord's grace.

Abram had a case of jaundice when he was born. I was a bundle of crashing hormones and a nervous wreck. The threat of him having to go back to the hospital was bringing back my anxiety. I remember one night crying in the shower with my husband just praying that the Lord would help his billirubin levels to go down. These were levels that caused his jaundice to proceed. Every day we would go to the doctor, and they would be rising. I prepared for the worst. That is when the Lord showed up. It is never our timing but His timing. The Lord had placed this miracle into my womb, and here I was worried about him having jaundice. The Lord always shows up. His jaundice levels went down, and I got to swallow some "humble pie" as I called it. My husband always told me that the Lord " had him", and I was too stubborn to realize it. I realized in a hurry that I wasn't in control. The Lord had brought us this far and here I was worrying.

Abram is healthy and absolutely perfect in every way. Sometimes I just stare at him and think how grateful I am. I mean I am so unworthy of anything, but the Lord gave us this bundle of joy. I am so thankful that he loves us unconditionally no matter what we do.

The Lord also knew when the time was right for Abram. My mother's sister Sherry, who is my aunt, was diagnosed with Stage 4 cancer. My grandmother, who I refer to as Nana, was absolutely devastated. This was her first child. Sherry had a very hard life not by anyone's fault but her own. We all have our vices that cause us hardship so I certainly won't point fingers. The bible talks about not judging anyone on this earth because we are all sinners. Everyone has different sins, but in the end they are all sins. Finding out that she had cancer really hit our family hard.

My grandmother always told me that Abram being born was her sanity. She had something to look forward to. Abram was her escape from the reality that she was facing of losing her child. I can't even imagine what she is going through. The thought of losing your child is horrific. My grandmother told me one time while we were riding in the car that she couldn't imagine what God felt when he sent Jesus to die on the cross. That was His one and only Son. It was a sad day, but I am so thankful that God loved us that much to send His son to die for our sins. Again, I say that we are so unworthy.

Again, I say that Abram being born was the perfect timing. My mom's boyfriend Scott had just lost his father to cancer. Scott lost his mother at a very young age, and his dad was never really around him his whole life. Scott tried to make amends with his dad and help him the last few years of his life. His dad was looking forward to seeing Abram. I remember when Abram was just born, and Scott got up at the dinner table and told us that Abram was such a blessing to him since he lost his dad.

I have no doubt in my mind that God gave us Abram at the right time for not just me and my husband but for everyone else as well. He knew what my family was going through and knew that we needed something so perfect to love and focus on through these times. I can't thank the Lord enough for the blessing that he has gave us. I hope and pray that everyone who wants a child will get to experience that love that I found with Abram. He is an absolute miracle. I take no credit for him because it was the Lord's will, timing, and unconditional love that brought him to us.

Thank you Lord for first loving us. Thank you Lord for giving me my story to tell others.

I take no credit for this book. This was the Lord's plan, and He inspired every bit of this book. I am so thankful to be given the opportunity to tell my story in hopes to help others understand the amazing love and power of God. Thank you Lord for choosing me to write this book.

Printed in the United States
By Bookmasters